Who Am I? II

Who Am I? II

Test Your *Biography* IQ

Based on the *Biography Magazine*
Column by David Goldman

**Andrews McMeel
Publishing**

Kansas City

00 01 02 03 04 RDC 10 9 8 7 6 5 4 3 2 1

Library of Congress Cataloging-in-Publication Data
Who am I? II : test your Biography I.Q. : based on the
Biography magazine column by David Goldman
     p. cm.
  ISBN 0-7407-0985-2 (pbk.)
    1. Biography—Miscellanea. I. Title: Who am I? two. II.
Goldman, David. III. Biography (Arts and Entertainment
Network)

CT105.W48 2000
920—dc21   00-030631

Design by Holly Camerlinck

For Kurt Rieschick, who started it all,
and all Kabrams and Goldmans,
past and present.

FOREWORD

A feature story in *Biography Magazine* examines the whole span of a person's life, with all its attendant ups and downs. But our *Who Am I?* column is a quick snapshot: We give you a few salient points, perhaps throw in some little-known details, leave out a few clues that would make the question too easy, then challenge you to identify the person. The mix of subjects is as eclectic as possible, ranging from the historical (Charlemagne) to the hysterical (Jerry Seinfeld) to both (George Burns).

The questions here have been especially created for this book—they've never appeared anywhere before. We invite you to challenge your memory, test your *Biography* IQ, and see how many of these famous folks you can identify.

—Paulette McLeod
Editor in Chief
Biography Magazine

The answer for each trivia question may be found on the page following the question.

1 **Although I was born in the Bronx, I spent the latter part of my life in England,** where I pursued my film career away from the glare of Hollywood. As a director, I'm a meticulous craftsman, and have been known to shoot the same scene dozens, if not hundreds of times. My films include *Dr. Strangelove* and *A Clockwork Orange;* a mystical outer space adventure was my biggest hit, and was named for the year that came thirty-three years after its release.

2 Although thirty-eight of my works survive today, I left no letters, and there is little known about my personal life. Leaving my hometown of Stratford-upon-Avon for London (some say because I stole a deer), I was a director and occasional actor when I wasn't writing works such as *Twelfth Night* and *Othello*. Many of my plays were staged at the courts of King James I and Elizabeth I, and are still performed today, almost four hundred years after my death. Some have been adapted into musicals and teen-oriented screen comedies.

3 **Although I was discouraged from going to college, I won an athletic scholarship to UCLA,** and then joined the Los Angeles police force. I served for over twenty years, and got my law degree during this time. I was defeated in my first mayoral run, but was successful four years later, when I became Los Angeles's first African-American mayor. The city grew during my twenty-year tenure, building its first international airport and hosting the Olympics.

4 When I left my wife in 1910, it made the front page of the *New York Times*. By then, I was a famous novelist and force for social change, setting up a school in my home for peasants, as well as a series of soup kitchens. I plagiarized Charles Dickens early in my career, but my reputation was made with *War and Peace* and *Anna Karenina*.

5 **I served my country as a minister overseas, in Berlin, St. Petersburg, and Holland,** before running for president in 1824, a job my father held decades before. But as president, I found that many of my ideas were not popular, including support for education and for a nationwide system of roads. After being defeated for reelection, I defended a group of escaped slaves in the Amistad case, and became the only former president to serve in the House.

Who Am I ?

6 **Although I was a mayor, newspaperman, and lecturer,** people nowadays associate my name with circuses. I was a master of publicity, exhibiting a "161-year-old" woman who claimed to be George Washington's nurse, as well as an actual mermaid. Despite these hoaxes, my museum and traveling circus were huge successes with the American public, featuring such attractions as General Tom Thumb and Jumbo the elephant. My circus was known as the "Greatest Show on Earth."

Much of my work in psychology was for the birds; that is, I trained pigeons to perform certain behaviors utilizing a system of rewards and punishments. I later tried the system on my children, building them a special playpen and designing toys that would stimulate their minds. My theory of behaviorism stated that what humans do was determined mostly by external stimuli, not by hidden, subconscious desires, a prominent idea in the 1950s and '60s.

8

My razor-sharp wit and tendency to poke fun at the powerful got me imprisoned twice in the Bastille. One of my favorite expressions translates as "Let us crush the infamous one," and I argued against religion, tyranny, and intolerance, in favor of a more enlightened view of the world. In fact, I was a leader of the Enlightenment, and believed literature should be a force in social change. A popular writer in my day (*Candide* is my best-known work), I died a wealthy man in 1778.

Who Am I?

9 **I am known as one of the great orators of American history;** Abraham Lincoln quoted me numerous times in the Lincoln-Douglas debates. I was Speaker of the House of Representatives and then one of the Senate's most powerful members: John C. Calhoun, Daniel Webster, and I were known as the "Great Triumvirate." A skilled negotiator, I helped bring about compromises that staved off the Civil War and helped preserve the Union, if only for a few more years. I died in 1852, before the country split apart.

Q.8 Voltaire

10 My parents were poor tomato farmers in the Bahamas, and while still in my teens, I dropped out of school to help them. After serving in the navy, I made my debut on Broadway with the American Negro Theater. My film career took off in the '60s with *Lilies of the Field* and *Guess Who's Coming to Dinner*. I am the first African-American to receive the American Film Institute's Lifetime Achievement Award.

11 Ever since our father gave us a toy that flew around the room, my brother and I had been fascinated with the possibilities of flight. My older brother studied every book he could get his hands on, and working in the back of our bicycle shop, we devised a vehicle that would make us airborne. With myself at the controls, we made our first flight, lasting twelve seconds, in 1903. When I died in 1948, our invention had changed the world, and perhaps made it a little smaller.

12

I was an Italian soldier with a love of the ladies until, while sick and imprisoned, I had a vision telling me I should get rid of my possessions and do good works. When I followed this path, my father disinherited me, but I went on to preach and help the less fortunate. I was canonized in 1228, two years after my death, and in 1980 Pope John Paul II named me the patron saint of ecologists.

13 In Concord, Massachusetts, I studied to be a preacher, but the death of my young wife caused me to reconsider my profession. My numerous essays (such as "Self-Reliance") and books began the Transcendentalist movement, in which individual intuition takes precedence over the rationalism of science. I was a friend to Henry David Thoreau, who lived in my house for a while.

14 Although I brought about a number of religious reforms, including the translation of some of the church service into English, I am remembered today for my many wives. It was the Pope's refusal to grant me a divorce from the first one that led me to establish the Church of England. Those who disagreed with this (as well as two wives) were executed.

15

I was born Steveland Morris in Detroit in 1950; I was blind from infancy. But I was a natural performer, playing harmonica, drums, and keyboards, and my first album touted me as "the 12-Year-Old Genius." When I was twenty-one, my label, Motown, granted me complete artistic control, and I produced, wrote, and performed my own material, on such albums as *Inner Visions* and *Songs in the Key of Life*. I was instrumental in having Martin Luther King Jr.'s birthday declared a national holiday.

16

Since I studied law, it was ironic that my notable invention was the subject of much legal trouble. Having lost a considerable amount of money in a patent fight over my cotton gin, I switched to manufacturing muskets for the government. In the process, I invented a procedure that would forever change manufacturing: standardized parts, with which the same item could be easily assembled, over and over again.

17 Even though I graduated last in my class at West Point, I had a reputation as both a brave and a lucky commander during the Civil War. Finding myself without a job after the war, I went west to fight Indian forces on the frontier. My luck ran out when I, along with hundreds of my men, was killed at Little Bighorn in 1876.

18

Even as a teen, I was already working on the project that would bring me fame: transmitting radio waves over long distances, without using telegraph wires. By age twenty-three I had succeeded, and in 1909 I shared the Nobel Prize in physics. My discovery paved the way for radio, and my experiments with microwaves might have led to the now-ubiquitous oven, had I lived past 1937.

19

My name now appears on milk cartons, thanks to the process I devised for heating liquids to eliminate harmful germs. I was obsessed with them, and was convinced they came from outside sources and didn't originate spontaneously in the body, as was commonly believed. Besides founding the science of microbiology, I developed vaccines against rabies and anthrax. In gratitude, my native France gave me a state funeral in 1895.

20

Today when people say that the end justifies the means, they are paraphrasing my ideas. My book *The Prince* is a textbook on how to get and retain power, using whatever unscrupulous methods are effective. The most important political figure of the Renaissance, I wrote on other topics, including the art of war, as well as a history of my native city, Florence.

21

I was a controversial but highly influential figure in the civil rights movement.

I held degrees from several universities, including Harvard, and helped found the National Association for the Advancement of Colored People in 1910, as well as editing its newsletter, *Crisis*. Persecuted for my political beliefs during the Cold War, I left the United States for Ghana, where I lived until my death in 1963.

22 **I joined the Milwaukee Braves in 1954, and moved with them to Atlanta.** It was there that I made history in 1974, when I broke Babe Ruth's career total of 714 home runs. By the time I retired in 1976, I'd hit 755; I also held the record for most times at bat, and greatest number of RBI's. I was elected to the Baseball Hall of Fame in 1982.

Who Am I ?

23

I helped westernize Russia, and under my reign we had our first navy and first native-language newspaper. I wrested power from the ruling autocrats, and was proclaimed emperor in 1721. I died four years later, after diving into ice-cold water to save some drowning soldiers.

24 Born and educated in Switzerland, I studied with Sigmund Freud, then broke with him because I thought he had sex on the brain. I founded the analytic school of psychology, which studied how human behavior is shaped by both thinking and feeling, as well as by the unconscious. I was the first to describe two familiar personality types: the introvert and the extrovert.

25 **After fighting in the Civil War, I attended Harvard Law School and wrote a book, *The Common Law*, which put forth my idea that the law is constantly evolving.** President Theodore Roosevelt appointed me to the Supreme Court in 1902, where I served until I was ninety-one. I was known for my liberal views, and my conflicts with my colleagues earned me the nickname "the Great Dissenter."

26 Before I helped change the image of the nursing profession, it was not considered a job for respectable women. I opened my first clinic in 1853 in Turkey during the Crimean War, during which I made vast improvements in both the standards of health care and the bureaucracy that dealt with it. Despite my image as "the lady with the lamp," I spent the rest of my life in semi-seclusion, hampered by illness and nerves, directing my organization and school from my London bed.

Q.26 Florence Nightingale

27

Contrary to my tough, streetwise screen image, I came from a well-off family and went to prep school (although I was thrown out). I was wounded while in the navy, leaving me with my characteristic tight-lipped style and slight lisp. All four of my wives were actresses; the last was Lauren Bacall. *The Maltese Falcon* and *Key Largo* are just two of my classic movies.

28

Millions of people felt my wrath as my armies swept across what is now China and Russia, slaughtering millions and destroying cities; some historians say the Middle East is now arid because I destroyed irrigation systems there. In 1215, I captured what is now Beijing, and my Mongol empire was one of the largest in history. But after my death in 1227, it was divided among my three sons, and gradually fell apart.

Who Am I ?

29

I studied jazz piano under greats like Fats Waller, and played in Kansas City with bands like the Blue Devils before forming my own. Billie Holiday and Lester Young are just two famous alumni of my band; we were also the first American group to give a command performance for the Queen of England. I'm famous for my swinging piano style and compositions like "One O'Clock Jump" and "April in Paris." (Alert jazz fans may have spotted me in *Blazing Saddles* as well.)

30

My "Little Red Book" is still read, and my presence is still felt in China.

After seizing power in 1949, I instituted major reforms, including the Great Leap Forward, an attempt to do away with private property and collectivize agriculture, and the Cultural Revolution, a movement to rid China of Western influences (such as rock 'n' roll and cosmetics). Although I made China into a world power, millions of people died as a result of my policies.

31

A Saxon monk born in 1483, I was appalled by many Church practices, including the granting of indulgences, whereby people paid to be absolved of sins. While some argue that I didn't actually tack ninety-five theses to the door of Wittenberg's castle church, their publication nevertheless started a revolution that would divide Christianity.

32

When I saw a "road roller" (a steam engine used for farm work) as a boy in Michigan, I was seized by the idea of building my own "horseless carriage." After years of research and development, my Model T automobile went on the market in 1908. Within a decade, I had the world's biggest car company and was world famous. I was a great philanthropist, as well as a prejudiced, paranoid tyrant.

Who Am I?

33

Although I was an ally of the United States during World War II, my later policies antagonized the West and brought on the Cold War. I was born Iosif Vissarionovich Dzhugashvili in Russia in 1879, and adopted my more well-known last name as a revolutionary; it means "man of steel." It is estimated I was responsible for the deaths of at least twenty million Russian people during my twenty-four-year reign.

Q.33 Joseph Stalin

34

I was the most famed performer of my day, both in my native France and around the world. I played numerous roles (including Hamlet, not an easy job for a woman), wrote plays, and owned theaters. Colorful both onstage and off (some say I slept in a coffin), I didn't let a leg amputation stop me from entertaining the troops during World War I.

35

To some, I'm no more than a terrorist, but my reputation has been somewhat rehabilitated in the last decade. Determined to oust Israel from my Palestinian homeland, for years my organization carried out raids, bombings, and assassinations. Forced to flee my Lebanon headquarters in 1982, I later acknowledged Israel's right to exist, and signed a peace agreement with Prime Minister Rabin in 1993 at the White House. I'm not always popular with my Arab colleagues either, especially when I supported Saddam Hussein during the Gulf War.

Q.34 Sarah Bernhardt

36 Top five things you should know about me: 1. I'm from Indiana; 2. I used to be a weatherman; 3. I once hosted the Academy Awards and was never asked back; 4. My mom has been a frequent guest on my late-night talk show; 5. I like to drive fast and have paid the consequences for it. Who Am I?

37

The first Russian ruler to be crowned as czar (in 1547), I strengthened the empire during the early part of my reign, annexing territories, making Moscow the capital, and convening a national assembly. My nickname comes from my habit of the casual torture and execution of my enemies (or those I perceived to be). In a fit of anger, I even killed my beloved son.

38

I never led troops into battle, but Winston Churchill called me "the organizer of victory" for World War II.

Having gained a reputation for brilliant battle planning during the first World War, I picked the generals who would help us defeat Germany and Japan, including Dwight Eisenhower. After the war, President Truman made me secretary of state, and named his European Recovery plan for me, a plan that probably saved the continent.

39 Born Lev Davidovich Bronstein in the Ukraine, I adopted my now-famous alias when I escaped from Siberian exile to help Lenin and my comrades establish the new Soviet state. I created and directed the Red Army, helping to win the civil war, but after a falling-out with Stalin found myself in exile again. I traveled to France and Turkey, while continuing to write my critiques of the new Soviet state, until I was murdered by a government assassin in Mexico in 1940.

Q.38 George Marshall

40

My success story is riveting, literally: it was that ingredient that helped ensure my fortune. I started a partnership with a tailor who'd come up with the idea of reinforcing the pockets of work pants with rivets. Our strong, sturdy denim jeans caught on with would-be gold rush prospectors, lumberjacks, and cowboys, and by 1880 my San Francisco–based company had over $2 million in sales. I died in 1902, but fifty years later my jeans would become part of mainstream America.

41

For someone who would make one of the most famous speeches in American history, I wasn't always so eloquent; while attending theological seminary, I got C's in public speaking. I was a pastor in a Montgomery church when I became involved with the attempt to integrate the buses there. Although it took nearly a year, we were successful, and my civil rights work continued in Selma, Birmingham, and across the South. Like many who strive for peace, I died violently, and today my birthday is a national holiday.

Who Am I?

42 I was Thomas Jefferson's neighbor and secretary, and he called on me to help explore the vast newly acquired territory west of Missouri. My partner and I set out from near St. Louis, and it took us one and a half years to reach the Pacific Ocean. Although we were not heard from for two years, we returned victorious in 1806, and I was named governor of the Louisiana territory. Three years later, while on my way to Washington to resolve a debt, I was found dead in an inn; whether it was murder or suicide is still open to debate.

43

After our 1905 art show, my colleagues and I were dubbed "the wild beasts" for our use of bright colors and distorted shapes. I fell into art at twenty, when my mother gave me some paints while I was recuperating from appendicitis. Toward the end of my life, when I was again bedridden, I turned to decoupage, cutting out shapes on colored paper and arranging them in a random but aesthetic manner. Picasso was a friend, and Gertrude Stein was an early patron of my work.

Q.42 Meriwether Lewis

44 After marrying and having children, I was a freelance writer for magazines when I began to be aware of "the problem that has no name"—the general dissatisfaction of many women with their domestic lives. After interviewing hundreds of women and sending out questionnaires to my Smith College classmates, I published *The Feminine Mystique* in 1963, a book that helped usher in the modern feminist movement in the United States. A founder and the first president of the National Organization for Women, I've recently written about society's attitudes toward aging.

45

Millions of people see my name every morning, without knowing who I was. I studied surgery at New York's Bellevue Hospital, and also had a keen interest in nutrition. While working at a sanatorium in Battle Creek, Michigan, I developed a healthy alternative to the breakfast tradition of eggs and bacon: little flakes made from corn. My brother Will started his own company in 1906 to market these and other cereals, and one of my patients, C. W. Post, had a similar idea.

4 6 My 1963 autobiography is *Portrait of Myself,* but I am better known for my pictures of Gandhi, Stalin, and innumerable working men and women, from South Africa to middle America. I covered World War II for *Life,* and my unforgettable images of the Deep South were collected in the book *You Have Seen Their Faces.* Fearless, I was not averse to climbing out on a ledge of the Chrysler Building or going on a bombing raid to get the shot I wanted.

Who Am I ?

Q.46 Margaret Bourke-White

47

In 1849, I was arrested, along with other political types, and charged with treason. Sentenced to a Siberian prison, I learned firsthand about the criminal mind, which would inform many of my novels. The most famous ones, which include *Crime and Punishment* and *The Brothers Karamazov,* were written in the last twenty years of my life, and deal with themes that remain relevant: alienation, the breakdown of society, and man's struggle for freedom. My work wasn't known in the English-speaking world until after my 1881 death.

I knew the rules of composition, yet dispensed with almost all of them. A major force in twentieth-century music, I incorporated numerous styles into my work, from dissonant atonalism to jazz. I've written opera, orchestra pieces, and a "Circus Polka" to be danced by elephants. One of my many ballets, *The Rite of Spring,* inspired a riot at its 1913 premiere; a few decades later, the music was used in a Disney film.

Q.48 Igor Stravinsky

49 Millions of viewers first saw me as a little girl with an alien friend, but my offscreen life wasn't as charmed. (Maybe I inherited some of this from my illustrious, and somewhat notorious, acting family.) By the time I was a teen, I was in and out of rehab, and by nineteen, I was divorced. But I've gotten back on track, appearing in a Woody Allen film, a Batman adventure, and the big-screen version of *Charlie's Angels*.

50 I abandoned a medical career to overthrow a government: China's Manchu dynasty. I traveled the world, both to study western politics and to drum up support. Our movement's "Three Principles of the People" were Democracy, Nationalism, and the People's Well-being. After many unsuccessful attempts, our revolt succeeded, and in 1911, I became president of the Chinese Republic.

Who Am I?

51

A drinking problem led to my resignation from the army in 1854, and my return to civilian life was not notable. But after the outbreak of the Civil War, I rejoined the army and distinguished myself as a commander in several battles. President Lincoln later made me head of the Union army, and after the war I was elected president. Although my time in office was marked by scandals, my memoirs (suggested by and perhaps contributed to by my friend Mark Twain) became a best-seller after my death.

52

I may be the most well-known stockbroker-turned-painter. After losing my original job in a stock market crash, I moved to Paris to paint; I also roomed with Vincent van Gogh. I abandoned my family for Tahiti, where I was inspired by its vibrant colors, lush landscapes, and enticing young girls, several of whom became my "wives." Although I blossomed as a painter, I wasted away as a human being, drinking, taking morphine, and dying of syphilis in 1903.

53

When I died in 1954, I was given a state funeral, the first French woman writer to be so honored. I scandalized society with my nearly naked stage appearances, had numerous affairs (with both men and women), and created the characters Claudine and Gigi. I was also a drama critic, reporter, and briefly had my own cosmetics company.

54 **I became head of the Chinese government in 1928.** After defeating Japanese forces during World War II, my nationalists battled the Communists for control of China. Driven out of the country in 1949, I set up a government in Taiwan. Harry Truman was no fan of mine, but with later U.S. support I was able to turn Taiwan into an industrialized nation with a booming economy.

55 To earn money to support my family, I started writing jokes and stories for newspapers, sometimes under the pen name "The Doctor Without Patients" (I was a medical student at the time). I continued to write stories, but my first play, *The Seagull*, was such a flop that I almost gave up playwriting. My plays favor character development over plot, mix humor with pathos, and deal largely with the declining power of the Russian gentry.

56 I was thrown out of military school, drank and used drugs, had bouts of insanity, and married my thirteen-year-old cousin. My calamitous life prevented me from becoming a wealthy writer, but I virtually invented the detective story with "Murders in the Rue Morgue," and turned out tales of horror and eerie poems such as "Annabel Lee." I died in 1849, shortly after being found drunk and disheveled in Baltimore, nevermore to write.

Who Am I?

57

I married my wife when I was thirteen, as was customary in my country. After living in South Africa for twenty years, fighting racial discrimination, I returned to India to work for independence. I maintained that my fellow Indian citizens should return to their simple, homegrown industries, and used a spinning wheel as a symbol of such self-sufficiency. Inspired in my nonviolent work by Tolstoy, I set up a cooperative farm in Johannesburg named after him.

58 The first movie I directed, *Grand Theft Auto,* was a low-budget action flick, but I've done a variety of films since, ranging from space adventures to romances to family-oriented comedies. I learned my craft from my acting family, and have been in the business since I was eighteen months old. Many people still know me as Andy Griffith's son and Fonzie's straitlaced friend.

59

As America's self-appointed moral conscience, I dispense advice to twelve million listeners on my daily radio show. In addition to a newspaper column, I've written several books, including *Ten Stupid Things Women Do to Mess Up Their Lives*. I am not a psychologist (I have a Ph.D. in physiology), but am known for my unyielding opinions on human behavior, as well as my continual reminder that "I am my kid's mom."

60 Until my death in 1918, I was the bare-knuckles champion of the world, and was known as the Boston Strong Boy. (My parents were Irish immigrants.) In 1882, however, I began using gloves, in accordance with the Queensbury Rules of Boxing. Ten years later, in the first heavyweight championship fight, I lost to Gentleman Jim Corbett in the twenty-first round. I am credited with helping to make boxing a popular U.S. sport.

61

I have stated that my life's goal is complete understanding of the universe, and have not let my condition hinder my study. For over thirty years, I've suffered from Lou Gehrig's disease, and am dependent on a wheelchair and a device that does my speaking for me. My book *A Brief History of Time* was a bestseller (complicated though it was), and made me a media celebrity; I've since appeared on *Star Trek: The Next Generation* and *The Simpsons*.

62

I was an opponent of both liquor and slavery, and formed the Women's Loyal League to eliminate the latter. My political goals expanded when I met Elizabeth Cady Stanton, and we started our women's suffrage organization. In the 1872 presidential election, I was arrested for trying to cast a ballot, and refused to pay the $100 fine. I died in 1906, fourteen years before my goal would be achieved.

Who Am I?

63 Born in Arizona in 1927, I was raised in migrant worker camps, and left school after sixth grade. After serving in the navy during World War II, I attempted to organize my fellow migrant laborers, and we eventually formed the United Farm Workers Union. I organized boycotts of grapes and lettuce to bring attention to our poor working conditions.

64

Early in my career, I appeared in films with both the Marx Brothers and the Three Stooges (I got hit by one of their pies). I did a radio show, *My Favorite Husband,* with my real-life spouse, before we moved on to television with a successful series. In 1953, the episode in which I had a baby was the highest-rated show in history. My last TV appearance, shortly before my death, was on the 1989 Academy Awards.

Many of the concepts I described in my work are now part of the language: the Oedipus complex, the "slip," the id, ego, and superego. I also began the practice of relaxing my psychiatric patients by putting them on a couch. By emphasizing how our unconscious impacts our everyday life, I forever changed the study of human behavior. Many of my theories remain controversial today (for one thing, I initially thought cocaine was a remedy for many ailments), more than sixty years after my death.

66 The first woman to serve as White House chief of protocol, I was also an ambassador to both Ghana and Czechoslovakia. But today people still remember me for my films, more than fifty years after I made my last one. Helping to lift America's spirits during the Depression, I received a special miniature Oscar (to match my small stature) in 1934, and a children's (nonalcoholic) cocktail was named after me.

67 I joined the Communist Party in 1961 (as a politician, I had no choice), and was in charge of housing for my province. My ability to get things done, despite the massive Soviet bureaucracy, brought me to the attention of President Gorbachev, who made me Moscow's party chief. Disillusioned, I quit the Communist Party in 1990 and, upon the breakup of the Soviet Union, became the first democratically elected Russian president. I was a hero when I stood up to Communist forces during an unsuccessful coup in 1991, but was later blamed for much of my country's economic troubles.

68 I began writing to support my family; my father was a philosopher who gave lectures and ran schools, but seemed clueless when it came to earning a living. Inspired by family friends like Emerson and Hawthorne, I wrote trashy stories like "Pauline's Passion and Punishment" and achieved literary success with a book on my experiences as a Civil War nurse. When a publisher wanted me to write a "girl's book," I came up with a novel loosely based on my family, *Little Women*.

Who Am I?

69 I am the only U.S. president with a Ph.D. I was president of Princeton University (my alma mater) before the local Democrats, impressed with my performance, persuaded me to run for governor of New Jersey. As president, I helped create the Federal Reserve System to stabilize the nation's banks, but my dream for a League of Nations wasn't realized in my lifetime, and while touring the country to promote it, I suffered a stroke. My wife performed many of my duties during my recovery.

70

How rich was I? In 1913, I was worth $1 billion, which translates to about $45 billion in today's dollars. I made my fortune in the oil business, and by the turn of the century controlled about 90 percent of the market, eventually incurring the wrath of the press and the scrutiny of the government. Before my death (at close to ninety-eight), I used much of my fortune to found New York's Riverside Church, a medical school, and several educational institutions.

71 **Although I was opposed to Communism, the Soviet government allowed me to work in their lab in 1935.** Perhaps it was because they were interested in my experiments in "conditioned responses"—whether behavior can be changed using scientific controls. I worked mainly with dogs, and my name may ring a bell with psychology students. For my physiology studies, I won the Nobel Prize in 1904.

A.70 John D. Rockefeller

72 After losing my job as editor of the *Brooklyn Eagle*, I held a series of odd jobs and continued to write. Ralph Waldo Emerson was an early champion of my work, but others found it immoral and vulgar (especially my candor about my homosexuality). During the Civil War, I was a nurse and wrote about my experiences, as well as a famed elegy to President Lincoln. Today my first book, *Leaves of Grass*, is still popular with both students and certain presidential interns.

73

Both in my work and in my life, I continually challenged society's assumptions about gender. At twenty-three, after getting my Ph.D. in anthropology, I journeyed to Samoa, and my study of the youth culture there became a best-selling book. I wrote several others exploring how gender is largely determined by culture, had a column in *Redbook* magazine, taught at Columbia University, and became the best-known social anthropologist of my day.

74

Religion and literature were my two interests; I combined both in much of my writing. My clergyman father moved us to Cincinnati, the farthest south I'd traveled up to that point. My most famous novel came to me in a vision. It dealt frankly with the harsh realities of slavery and further spurred on the abolitionist movement. When President Lincoln met me, he asked, "Is this the little woman who made this great war?"

75 In an essay, I once suggested (facetiously) a solution to Irish poverty: have the poor feed their babies to the rich. It was hardly something you would expect from a clergyman, but that was just one example of my savagely satiric writing. I was a hero in my native Dublin, where my birthday was celebrated with bell ringing. My 1726 novel *Gulliver's Travels* is now a popular children's story, but it's actually a biting commentary on the absurdities of mankind.

Who Am I?

Q.74 Harriet Beecher Stowe

76

Growing up a poor country boy, I knew hard times: my twin brother died at birth, my father spent time in jail, and afterward he didn't always have a job. At eighteen, while working as a truck driver, I went into a small studio in Memphis to make a record for my mama. The owner was impressed and had me record some more songs, and by 1955, I was a national sensation; a few years later, I was a movie star. The palatial home I bought in Memphis, Graceland, is now a major tourist attraction. I left this world in 1977, according to most people.

77

I was part of Ralph Waldo Emerson's Transcendentalist group, and in 1845 I built a cabin on some land he owned. I lived there for two years, chronicling my life and my observations of nature. I also spent a night in jail for refusing to pay a tax to support the Mexican War, a position I defended in my famous essay "Civil Disobedience." My work sold poorly, and most of it wasn't published during my lifetime. I held a series of other jobs (including working in my family's pencil business) before dying of tuberculosis at forty-five.

78

Before I became one of the twentieth century's most infamous figures, I was a schoolteacher and a journalist for a socialist paper. But my politics did an about-face, and my Fascist Party was running Italy by 1926. My governing abilities (it's said I made the trains run on time) brought praise from Winston Churchill, among others, but my downfall was joining Hitler to fight the Allies during World War II. After losing power and escaping to Switzerland, I was shot, along with my mistress, by Italian partisans.

79

Many people remember me for introducing tobacco to the colonies, but there was more to me than just smoke. A favorite at Queen Elizabeth's court, I helped found the first English colony in the New World. It was on Roanoke Island in what is now North Carolina. (It didn't last, since the colonists were more interested in gold.) I fell out of favor when James I ascended the throne, and while imprisoned for treason, wrote a history of the world and several poems. When I was finally released, I went on my own search for gold (in what later became Venezuela), but after fighting with the Spanish, I returned to England and was beheaded for my bad behavior.

80 **Taking photographs was a bulky, laborious process until I set about finding an easier way.** By 1888, my associates and I had invented a portable camera, giving it a made-up name I thought would be easy to remember: Kodak. By the turn of the century, my company was producing photographic equipment, as well as motion picture film for Thomas Edison. I gave away about $75 million of my fortune before ending my life in 1932; I left a note saying my work was done.

Who Am I ?

81

Corn would lead to my scientific breakthrough, although no one believed it at first. A solitary child who loved science and reading, I studied botany and genetics at college. I became interested in chromosomes and how they affected heredity, and while everyone else was using fruit flies, I studied color patterns in Indian corn kernels, gradually discovering that genes can change their positions in chromosomes. It would take years for my findings to be accepted, but by the 1960s and '70s I had received numerous awards for my work, and in 1983 was the first woman to win an unshared Nobel Prize in physiology and medicine.

82

I got my big break in a "Mr. Universe" contest in London in 1953. I came in third, and an impressed casting director put me in the chorus line of *South Pacific*. My subsequent roles have been nonmusical, including an aging Robin Hood and Indiana Jones's father, but I'll forever be linked with a name and a number: 007. Despite my outspoken support for Scotland, I was recently knighted by Queen Elizabeth.

Q.81 Barbara McClintock

83 **Shortly after becoming the army's chief of staff, I led the right-wing forces to victory in the Spanish Civil War of 1936–39, with help from Hitler and Mussolini.** I kept my country out of World War II, and although I did eliminate many political enemies, in the 1950s and '60s my repressive regime loosened up a bit, and Spain prospered. I died in 1975, but *Saturday Night Live* continually gave updates on my condition for months afterward.

84

My father said that he'd rather see me dead than an artist, but I defied him and moved to Paris to paint. The only American among the Impressionists (and the only woman), I used my family as subjects, and favored scenes of mothers and babies. I also aided my colleagues by directing rich American patrons to the one dealer who sold the Impressionists' work. I received France's Legion of Honor award in 1904.

85

I was a male war bride; that is, I was one in the movies. After a stint as a juggler in a traveling acrobatic troupe, I got a break when Mae West cast me in one of her films; I later played opposite Katharine Hepburn, Myrna Loy, and Grace Kelly. A dashing, suave leading man, I also starred in such Hitchcock thrillers as *Notorious* and *North by Northwest*.

86 While still in Harvard Medical School, I was writing fiction under the pen name John Lange, churning out (by my own estimation) thousands of words a day. Much of my work deals with science and technology gone amok, but I've also written an autobiography and a book on painter Jasper Johns, and adapted my books *Rising Sun* and *Disclosure* for the screen. By the '90s, I had penned dozens of best-sellers and blockbuster films, and created the hit medical drama *ER*.

87

I first performed with the group Miami Latin Boys at a wedding, and we went on to be a top recording act after we changed our name. Our first hit, "Conga," was one example of the Latin-accented pop that's made me a top recording star. I continue to support my adopted hometown of Miami, and organized a benefit concert for the victims of Hurricane Andrew in 1992. I made my film debut with Meryl Streep in *Music of the Heart*.

88

My family was not particularly religious, but after reading Dickens and other socially conscious writers, I got more involved in the affairs of my fellow man. I wrote for a socialist paper, trained to be a nurse, and friends and I started a Christian-oriented newspaper, *The Catholic Worker*. During the Depression, we operated "houses of hospitality" for the poor across the country. Mother Teresa is just one of the people who has called me "saintly," but my frequent criticisms of the Church may stall my canonization.

89 **Born in the United States to an Irish mother and a Spanish father, I would play a crucial role in the struggle for Irish independence.** Active in Sinn Fein, I was arrested and imprisoned several times for my activities, and in 1918 escaped to the United States to drum up support. Elected president of the government in exile, I opposed a 1922 treaty with Britain that I felt gave us a raw deal (and was imprisoned again). Under our new constitution in 1937, I was elected Ireland's first prime minister, and later, its president.

90

I was born in New York, but moved to Italy with my husband, hoping to cure his tuberculosis. When he died, I was faced with caring for our five children, and was taken in by my husband's friends. Inspired by their faith and charity, I converted to Roman Catholicism and started my own order of nuns in Emmitsburg, Maryland, to help the needy. In that city I also opened the first Catholic school, beginning the country's parochial school system. In 1975, more than 150 years after my death, I became the first American-born saint.

Q.89 Eamon De Valera

91

My ancestors took part—on the side of the accusers—in the Salem witch trials of the seventeenth century, and the guilt this caused me informed much of my writing. For children, I wrote a history of my native New England and several books of stories, and even penned a biography of my friend Franklin Pierce for his presidential campaign. (After his election, he named me consul to Liverpool and Manchester.) My best-known work, *The Scarlet Letter,* is another tale of moral conflict, telling of a young Puritan woman who must pay the price for her adultery.

My show business career lasted longer than most people's lives. I was a vaudeville performer, a TV and radio star, producer, and singer (some people would question that last one). In 1975, I made my first movie in thirty-six years and won an Oscar for it. I went on to play God and an elderly bank robber, and died in 1996, just after my one-hundredth birthday.

93 In 1961, after being ordained, I joined another famous minister, Martin Luther King Jr., in his civil rights fight, and later became executive director of his Southern Christian Leadership Conference. After Dr. King's assassination in 1968, I entered politics, and was elected to Congress as a representative from Georgia. I was an outspoken ambassador to the United Nations (the first African-American to hold that post) and served as mayor of Atlanta.

94

I was born Eric Arthur Blair in India in 1903, the son of a British civil servant, and, lacking the finances to go to Oxford or similar schools, joined the Burmese Imperial Police. This later became the basis for a book, as did my experiences fighting in the Spanish Civil War. I returned from Spain disillusioned with much of the Communist movement, and wrote my two best-known novels, both about the horrors of totalitarianism. One featured talking barnyard animals; the other was a futuristic nightmare in which Big Brother watched over us all.

95 I attended military school (a fine beginning for a protest singer) and studied journalism before falling in with the Greenwich Village folk scene of the 1960s.

Frequently compared to the work of Bob Dylan, my songs focused on issues of the day, such as the Vietnam War and civil rights; they include "I Ain't Marchin' Anymore" and "Draft Dodger Rag." I later did an about-face into '50s-style rock, appearing onstage at Carnegie Hall in a gold lamé suit, and getting booed by outraged fans. Despondent and battling depression, I committed suicide in 1976.

96 Given my background, it's amazing that I became a humorist: after my mother was institutionalized, I lived in a series of orphanages and foster homes. In 1942, I quit high school and joined the army, and it was while I was posted on a Pacific island and afterward in college that I discovered a talent for writing. After the war, I lived in Paris, writing for the *International Herald Tribune* about the local nightlife. In 1962, I returned to the United States, settling in Washington to write the political humor column for which I am now famous.

97

Q.96 Art Buchwald

In 1841, I started the *New York Tribune*, served as editor, and became an influential voice, speaking out for labor unions, the welfare of the common man, and the abolition of slavery. I never became wealthy, possibly because I had the radical notion of letting some employees share in the company's profits. I ran unsuccessfully for president against Ulysses S. Grant, and was a popular lecturer around the United States. It was during my travels that I no doubt realized that a young man's fortune might be ensured if he were to "Go west."

98 **My grandfather, for whom I am named, was a former slave and Civil War soldier, and my mother was among the first black graduates of Columbia Teachers College.** After graduating first in my class from Howard University Law School, I became the lawyer for the NAACP, and argued in front of state and federal courts, as well as the Supreme Court. In 1967, I was appointed to the Court by President Johnson, where I continued to champion the rights of the poor and minorities and spoke out against the death penalty.

Who Am I?

99

I was the original gangster hoofer. After an inauspicious start as a female impersonator, I made my Broadway debut in a chorus line, and showed off my dancing skills in other films. My first of many tough-guy parts was 1931's *Public Enemy* (in which I had a memorable scene with a grapefruit), but I've also played George M. Cohan (in two films), Lon Chaney, and a Shakespearean ass. Offscreen, I helped found the Screen Actors Guild.

100

For someone who started off in Staten Island with just one tugboat, I did pretty well. After running freight and passenger service to Manhattan, I established my own steamship company. The California gold rush paid off for me, as I developed faster ships to run the New York–to–San Francisco route (via Nicaragua). I then invested my substantial fortune in railroads, and by 1867 controlled the New York Central line. At the time of my death, I was worth about $100 million; I took 1 percent of that to create the Tennessee university that bears my name.

101

One of my main objectives as Soviet premier was attempting to eliminate the worst excesses of my predecessor, Joseph Stalin. I planned for the Soviet Union to defeat the West not through war but through demonstrating the superiority of Communism over capitalism. (Not that I didn't lose my temper now and then, as I showed in my famous shoe-banging performance at the United Nations.) I encouraged greater agricultural production, visited America, launched the space program, and sent missiles to Cuba, which were sent back after a tense standoff with President Kennedy. This setback, as well as the failure of my domestic policies, led to my ouster in 1964.

102

I yearned to be a soldier like my late father, but there weren't any battles of note in my native France in the late eighteenth century. So at nineteen, defying a government ban, I set sail for America to join in the colonies' revolution. John Adams admired me; after contributing millions of dollars to the American cause I was made a general, and served with George Washington. Together we won the Battle of Yorktown, and I was celebrated as a national hero. My role in the subsequent French Revolution made me the "Hero of Two Worlds."

103

An engineer, writer, poet, and philosopher, I believed many of the world's problems could be solved through better-designed, more efficient housing for all mankind. The geodesic dome is my most famous accomplishment, a self-supporting structure made up of tetrahedrons (four-sided pyramids) that can easily be taken apart and reassembled. I designed one for the Ford company, and another was at the U.S. pavilion at Expo '67 in Montreal. Other inventions: a flat world map that can be folded into a makeshift globe, and a three-wheeled, energy-efficient car.

104

I was so embarrassed by my first role in a movie that I took out an ad in a trade paper asking people not to watch it when it was shown on television. I improved from there, in films like *Hud, Harper,* and *The Hustler* (not all my films begin with the same letter). I was nominated multiple times for an Oscar before I actually won. Today, many people recognize my name (and face) from my line of salad dressings, popcorn, and spaghetti sauces.

Who Am I?

105

My sister and I started singing in Ohio in the 1940s, and when she retired I continued, as one of many girl singers of the period. (In fact, *Girl Singer* is my recent autobiography.) My first hit was the novelty song "Come On-a My House," but I've since recorded more substantial material. I've appeared in films (including *White Christmas*) as well as on *ER*, which starred my famous nephew.

106

I was captivated by the blues at an early age, and soon was learning classics by Robert Johnson and Muddy Waters on my guitar. I left the British group The Yardbirds when I thought we were becoming too commercial, and played in Cream and Blind Faith before going solo in the 1970s. I've composed music for films, appeared in the movie *Tommy,* and my unmistakable lead guitar can be heard on the Beatles' "While My Guitar Gently Weeps."

107

Teaching in Goshen, New York, during Revolutionary times, it bothered me that all my textbooks were English. What was needed, I felt, were books that reflected the American way of speech. In 1783, I put out my own spelling book, and later discussed with my friend Benjamin Franklin how to simplify the subject (for example, taking the silent letters from words like *bread* and *friend*). For twenty years I worked on my massive project, *An American Dictionary of the English Language,* a two-volume reference work containing more entries than any other dictionary. My name is still found on updated versions.

108

I came from a prominent Kentucky family, and was living in Illinois when I married my famous husband in 1842. I've been portrayed somewhat unfairly as shrewish and insane, but it's evident that the traumas I endured added to my fragile mental condition. I was with my husband when he was assassinated, and lost three of my four sons, one while we were living in the White House.

Who Am I?

109 My parents ran a theater school, so perhaps it was inevitable that I join the family business. My brother, also an actor, helped me get a part in my first movie; then I got noticed with a role in the ensemble comedy *Mystic Pizza*. I've since played a kindhearted hooker, Tinkerbell, and a reluctant bride. In real life, I had a brief marriage to a country singer/actor, and I've been linked romantically with several of my costars.

110 In 1831, I left France for America, ostensibly to study the country's prisons. Traveling from Boston to New Orleans, I observed how its political and social forces affected the nation's population. (Among my observations: majority rule could be as bad as that of a dictator, and the most able men do not always run things.) My book *Democracy in America* remains a valuable political text.

111

I was with Chairman Mao on his Long March, but was put under house arrest during his Cultural Revolution. After his death I worked to bring China into the twentieth century, emphasizing science and technology (many students were sent to the United States to study). I also toured the United States and negotiated with Britain on the return of Hong Kong to Chinese control. Despite my efforts to discontinue the ruthless brutality of my predecessor, I nevertheless ordered the massacre of students during the 1989 pro-democracy demonstrations in Tiananmen Square.

Q.110 Alexis de Tocqueville

112 Before becoming my country's leader in 1979, I had a seat in Parliament and served as minister for education and science (where I provoked outrage by getting rid of the free milk program in schools). Like my American counterpart, who served at about the same time as I did, my aim was to reduce the role of government, dismantling the welfare state and privatizing many nationalized industries. When I resigned in 1990, I had served longer than any British prime minister in this century.

113 I began working on the H-bomb for the KGB, but by 1961 I was protesting its **atmospheric testing.** Abandoning science to work for peace, I spoke out for nuclear disarmament, and won the Nobel Peace Prize in 1975. I wasn't allowed to leave Russia to receive it, and in 1980 was sent into exile in the city of Gorky. I was finally allowed to return to Moscow in 1986, and continued my human rights work until my 1989 death.

114

In the 1950s, I was a popular gospel singer, and released my first pop song under another name so as not to alienate my fans. I finally left my group, the Soul Stirrers, to write and record soul and R&B classics such as "You Send Me" and "Cupid." I was one of the first black music entrepreneurs, with my own record label and publishing company. "A Change Is Gonna Come," an unofficial civil rights anthem, was released after my 1964 death.

115 **My political career began when I rang doorbells for Barry Goldwater's 1964 presidential campaign in my Chicago suburb.** When I graduated Wellesley, I spoke at commencement (the first student ever to do so) and moved on to Yale Law School, where I met my future husband, as well as Marian Wright Edelman, president of the Children's Defense Fund. I briefly worked for her organization, and remain an advocate for children's issues, as in my 1996 book, *It Takes a Village*.

116 While I've been lampooned for my supercilious speaking style and verbiage, I remain an erudite spokesperson for the right. After matriculation at Yale, I launched the conservative publication the *National Review* in 1955, and began hosting my television program *Firing Line* the decade after. Not that I'm circumscribed by political matters: I've penned numerous espionage novels, as well as a best-seller on a favorite nonlucrative occupation: sailing.

117 After graduating from the U.S. Military Academy, I was an aide to my father (a former Civil War general) and President Theodore Roosevelt, as well as being the army's first public relations officer. I was a national hero for my command of the Southwest Pacific forces during World War II, but during the Korean conflict I faced opposition to my plan to move the war into China, and was relieved of my command. I returned to my beloved country to a tumultuous reception, and in my farewell speech to Congress I told them that "old soldiers never die, they just fade away."

118 One of a set of triplets, I left home instead of taking the job intended for me as my father's bookkeeper. Although I planned to be a pediatrician, I found my calling as a psychiatrist in Chicago, where I worked with terminally ill patients. My book *On Death and Dying* examined this once-taboo issue, even naming the five stages a person with a fatal illness goes through: denial, anger, bargaining, depression, and acceptance.

Who Am I?

119

Had it not been for a high school wrestling injury, I might have had a different career. Sidelined from the team, I auditioned for my school's production of *Guys and Dolls,* and got cast as Nathan Detroit. Bitten by the acting bug, I left school and soon got cast in several films. But it wasn't until a scene where I danced around in my underwear to a Bob Seger song that I really got noticed. My costars have included my wife, Paul Newman, Dustin Hoffman, and Jack Nicholson.

Q.118 Elisabeth Kübler-Ross

120

Although I had little formal schooling after age fourteen, I became one of Britain's major Victorian-era poets. One of my early works, "Pippa Passes," deals with a little Italian girl and her effect on passersby. I married Elizabeth Barrett, a better-known poet than myself, in 1846, and we moved to Italy both for her health and to get away from her disapproving family. Our happy union lasted just sixteen years, and after her death I produced my greatest work, *The Ring and the Book,* an epic poem told by the various characters in an Italian murder trial.

121

After serving in the Soviet army, I was exiled to a work camp for some anti-Stalin comments I'd written to a friend. I wrote my novel *One Day in the Life of Ivan Denisovich*, about one inmate's experiences, and continued to expose the horrors of the Russian system in books like *The Gulag Archipelago*. The USSR took away my citizenship in 1974, four years after I won the Nobel Prize in literature. I lived in Vermont for twenty years and was finally able to return to my homeland in 1994, which I found almost unrecognizable.

122

Like my older brother, I was a naval officer, and my exploits included fighting pirates in the West Indies and capturing Veracruz in the Mexican War. But my most historic accomplishment was in 1853, when four of my ships sailed into Tokyo Bay to present Japan's emperor with several petitions, including protection for shipwrecked sailors and the right to buy coal. It opened up the mysterious country to the West for the first time since the seventeenth century.

123

In 1980, a group of sportswriters named me Athlete of the Century. I grew up in Brazil, where soccer is a way of life, and by age seventeen had led my country's team to the first of our three World Cup championships. In my twenty-two-year career, I scored 1,281 goals, and at one point was the highest-paid athlete in the world. I was born Edson Arantes do Nascimento, but millions of fans know me by my one-word nickname.

Q.122 Matthew Calbraith Perry

124

In 1977, I became the first western rock star to tour the Soviet Union, but by then the rest of the world was very familiar with me. While still a lad (and using my real name of Reginald Dwight), I won a piano scholarship to the Royal Academy of Music. I paid my dues playing in bars before hooking up with lyricist Bernie Taupin, who would be my collaborator for most of my career. Although I'm famed for my extravagant eyewear and outrageous stage costumes, I'm capable of quiet tunes like "Your Song" and "Can You Feel the Love Tonight."

125

Although I was not a successful businessman, my invention would later prove very useful. While in jail for debt, I began experimenting to find a way to improve rubber. When I mixed it with sulfur I discovered vulcanization, a process that made it more durable. I wrote a book on rubber (literally—some copies were printed on it) to promote this miraculous substance, but I endured years of legal trouble over my patents, and died poor in 1860.

126

Was it art? That's what critics and the public wanted to know about my work. I studied at the Art Students League in New York with Thomas Hart Benton, and many of my early paintings, like his, were of realistic American scenes. But in 1947, I began dripping paint on canvases, using sticks or trowels, to create a new kind of abstract painting. At my first show of these "splatter paintings," only one sold, for $150. I died in a drunk-driving accident in 1956, and my work now sells for millions.

127

I wrote about the emptiness of the modern world in poems like "The Waste Land" (wherein I stated that April is the cruelest month) and "The Love Song of J. Alfred Prufrock." The unconventional structure of that work (my publisher wasn't sure it was poetry, and held on to it for a year) changed and revitalized English literature. I also wrote literary criticism and several plays, and today my work lives on as the source material behind the world's longest-running musical (featuring a bunch of singing cats).

Q.126 Jackson Pollock

Who Am I?

128 I found my calling in jail. In 1841, I taught a Sunday school class in a Massachusetts prison and discovered women who were obviously mentally ill among the inmates. Finding similarly horrifying conditions (including chained patients) in other jails, I petitioned the state legislature to create separate facilities for these unfortunate individuals. I opened the first mental hospital in Trenton, New Jersey, and my crusade extended to many other states, as well as Europe. My only break was during the Civil War, when I was superintendent of nurses for the Union army.

129 At eighteen, I was on the cover of *Seventeen,* but my modeling career came second to my musical one. My mother was a gospel singer and I joined her in our church choir; I also got tips from my cousin Dionne Warwick. My self-titled debut album was released in 1985, and sold twenty-two million copies. I made my film debut with Kevin Costner, playing (what else?) a singer.

130

My blooming career started in Massachusetts, where, inspired by Darwin's theory of natural selection, I bred new strains of plants. A new, hardier potato was my ticket to success. I sold the rights to it and moved to California, where I continued to develop new types of plants, vegetables, and fruits, including the plumcot—a cross between a plum and an apricot. At the time of my death in 1926, I still had three thousand experiments under way, and today that potato, as well as a California city, is named for me.

131

I left Pennsylvania to move to Paris in 1903, where I spent the rest of my life. My unconventional writings, in which I played around with the English language, included verse, novels, and operas, as well as the autobiography of my longtime companion, Alice B. Toklas. Our apartment became a meeting place for many artists and writers, including Hemingway, Picasso, and Matisse. To describe the many American expatriates who came to Paris after the Great War, I coined the phrase "Lost Generation."

132

It's a story that's now become myth, but it happened to me. While I was at Coney Island, a burly lifeguard kicked sand in my face and stole my girlfriend. That was the motivation I needed to build up my scrawny physique, and I created a program of "Dynamic Tension" to do that. Changing my name from Angelo Siciliano (I was born in Italy) to that of a Greek hero, I sold my exercise regimen through mail order; generations of readers saw the ads in the backs of comic books.

133

I've played the Elephant Man on Broadway and a space alien on-screen, but I'm known mainly as a rock star of many faces. I spent time in a monastery and studied mime before breaking into music; an early hit, "Space Oddity," tied in with the first moon-landing. I later abandoned my space-age, androgynous image to record soul and electronic-influenced rock, and sang "The Little Drummer Boy" with Bing Crosby on his last Christmas special. I've also collaborated with John Lennon, Mick Jagger, and Queen.

134

While attending Harvard Law School, I wrote about the dangers of American automobiles, and while at the Department of Labor published a report that later became my 1965 book, *Unsafe at Any Speed.* This attack on the auto industry's lax safety standards led to legislation as well as the beginnings of the consumers' rights movement. My "Raiders" and I continue to fight for environmental safety, health care, and the rights of consumers against mighty corporations.

135 **I was born in Texarkana, Texas, the son of a former slave.** After teaching myself piano, I went to St. Louis, where I wrote and performed my own compositions. My black American folk opera, *Treemonisha,* flopped at its 1915 premiere, and I died soon after. In 1973, there was a revival of interest in my music after it was featured on the soundtrack of the Oscar-winning movie *The Sting.*

136

I was one of the biggest recording artists of the 1970s. I left the Chad Mitchell Trio folk group to go solo, and changed my last name from Deutschendorf to that of a well-known western metropolis. Many of my songs celebrate the wide-open spaces of the west, and the governor of Colorado named me the state's poet laureate. I wrote "Leaving on a Jet Plane" for Peter, Paul and Mary, while my own hits include "Calypso" and "Annie's Song." I died in 1997 in the crash of a small plane I was piloting.

Who Am I?

137

Despite little formal education, I was one of the most influential women of my day, an advocate of equal rights for women (especially education) and a foe of slavery. I was frequently separated from my husband, who was away in Congress or in Europe on diplomatic missions, and our letters, published posthumously in the 1840s, provide a personal look into eighteenth-century life. I was first lady, but died several years before my son also became president.

138

With about twenty thousand total works to my credit, I am one of the most prolific artists in history. My output includes paintings, sculptures, lithographs, etchings, and ceramics. In my "blue period," I utilized that color to paint melancholy scenes, while my experiments in cubism fragmented the traditional view of an object. One of my well-known works is a huge mural, inspired by the German bombing of the town of Guernica during the Spanish Civil War.

139

I liked to hunt, I liked to fish, and I liked to write. I was married four times, and had affairs with many women. I loved to watch men battle bulls, and described it in *Death in the Afternoon*. Later, I wrote a book about an old man trying to catch a fish. I lived in Cuba for twenty-two years, and that was good. Then I moved to Idaho, where I shot myself with my shotgun.

140

I grew up in Peekskill, New York, until my dad moved my nine siblings and me to Australia, partly thanks to money he won on *Jeopardy!* A hard-drinking, brawling guy, I went to one audition still showing wear and tear from a recent fight. The director decided I was perfect for the title role in *Mad Max*. I've played my share of action heroes, but have also starred as Hamlet, and won an Oscar for directing.

Who Am I?

141

My auto-biography was called *Maybe I'll Pitch Forever,* and I almost did. In 1965, I became the oldest person ever to play in a major league ball game. (I was about fifty-nine; my exact date of birth is open to question.) I started in the Negro Leagues, and traveled the world in the off-season, pitching in Canada, the Caribbean, and South America. In 1948, I was finally admitted to the major leagues (as baseball's oldest rookie) and played for the Cleveland Indians.

142

I commanded the French army in Italy, in 1796, and three years later my forces and I took France, where I was installed as leader. (I was named emperor in 1804.) I hired writers and artists to write about and glorify my exploits, and under my reign, French laws were standardized and civil liberties and freedom of religion were guaranteed. My armies conquered most of Europe and Egypt, before I met my defeat in Belgium. My presence is still felt in France; one physical legacy is the Arc de Triomphe, whose inner walls contain the names of my generals and famous battles.

143

My auntie, who raised me in postwar Liverpool, told me I would never earn a living with a guitar. But my mates and I persisted, and soon our little group was a bigger hit than we'd ever imagined. After my avant-garde artist wife and I married, we staged "bed-ins" for peace; I later made solo albums and moved to New York City. I retired from public life in 1975 to raise my son Sean, who is now a recording artist as well. In 1980, I was shot to death outside my apartment building in New York City.

Q.142 Napoleon Bonaparte

144

I escaped from a life of slavery in 1838, and three years later, my impromptu speech at an abolitionist conference in Massachusetts established me as an eloquent speaker for the cause. My famous autobiography was published in 1845, the same year I went to England to escape my country's Fugitive Slave Laws. After my supporters purchased my freedom, I campaigned for President Lincoln and helped form two regiments of black soldiers during the Civil War. Several years before my death, I served as U.S. minister to Haiti.

145 For someone whose discoveries would change the world, my early life wasn't promising: I didn't speak till age three, and did poorly in school, even dropping out several times. My theories on relativity and the particle nature of light revolutionized physics and I won the Nobel Prize in that field in 1921. An outspoken pacifist and Zionist, I was offered the presidency of Israel, which I turned down. When Hitler came to power, I left my native Germany for the United States, and died in Princeton, New Jersey, in 1955.

146

In 1990, one of my paintings sold for more than $82 million; I never sold more than two of them during my lifetime. I was a colleague of Pissarro and Toulouse-Lautrec and a roommate of Paul Gauguin. My paintings include several self-portraits and *Starry Night*; *Wheat Field with Crows* was the last I completed before my 1890 suicide.

Who Am I ?

147

In my autobiography, *The Road Ahead*, I wrote about my new house in the Northwest. The living space is "about average," and includes an indoor pool, a movie theater, and a banquet hall that can accommodate one hundred guests. I dropped out of college in 1975 to start a computer company with a friend. Sensing a window (or Windows) of opportunity, we focused on software instead of hardware. Our operating system (which became the standard for most computers), and the various applications of it, enabled us to grow and prosper, earning praise from computer novices, anger from envious competitors, and scrutiny from the Justice Department.

148

My mother was American and my father was English, and my tenacity and rousing speeches **helped Britain keep its spirits up during the dark days of World War II.** I served my country as a member of Parliament and secretary of war before becoming prime minister. After being defeated for another term, I warned of the "Iron Curtain" (a phrase I helped popularize) descending on Europe, then was reelected in 1951. I spent my later years painting and writing, and was made an honorary U.S. citizen by an act of Congress in 1963.

149

Historical opinion on me is mixed: Many see me as a power-mad dictator, but others claim I instituted many important reforms and was a great military leader, second only to Alexander the Great.

I did away with Rome's unfair tax system, installed Cleopatra as Queen of Egypt, and reformed the calendar to make it more accurate. (I should have left out the Ides of March, however.) As I had no male heirs, my grandnephew, Octavius, became Rome's first emperor after my death.

150 **I worked as an electrician in a Polish shipyard, but was fired in 1976 for my role in antigovernment protests.** Four years later, I was able to successfully organize my fellow workers, and we went on strike. Under martial law, the Polish government suspended our Solidarity union, but in 1989 we helped form a coalition government, and the following year I was elected president of Poland in a landslide. I tried to bring reform to the country, and encouraged a market economy, but facing increasing opposition by voters, I was defeated in 1995.

151

I was born in a crossfire hurricane . . . well, no, but it's the opening line of one of my famous songs.
I grew up middle-class in postwar England, attended the London School of Economics, and struck up a friendship with a fellow blues fan that led to our famous band. Although I've done solo albums and acted in films, I'm best known as the lead singer of the self-proclaimed "world's greatest rock 'n' roll band."

Q.150 Lech Walesa

152 I left my native Boston for Philadelphia, where I started a fire company, a university, and what was probably the country's first public library. I served my country as a diplomat, spending years abroad in England and France, as well as helping to draft both the Declaration of Independence and the Constitution. Today people remember me for my role in the American Revolution, for my stove, and for that experiment with the kite.

153

Unlike most other actors, I was popular in high school (in suburban New Jersey), and was both a cheerleader and homecoming queen. After studying at Vassar and Yale, I won an Emmy for my role in the miniseries *Holocaust*, then moved on to star with Dustin Hoffman, Robert Redford, and Clint Eastwood. I've played a variety of characters with a variety of accents (Australian, French, Italian) and been rewarded with two Oscars.

154

Although I was a multimillionaire, I had some help: I inherited much of my wealth from my father, who invented a bit used in oil drilling. I owned the RKO Movie Studio, Trans World Airlines, hotels, casinos, and real estate. A dashing bachelor in the 1930s (whose girlfriends included Katharine Hepburn and Joan Crawford), at the time of my death in 1976 I was an eccentric, drug-addicted, ninety-three-pound recluse.

155

By the age of six, I was supporting my family, traveling all over Europe performing for royalty. (I was skilled on the clavier, violin, and organ.) By eight, I had written my first symphony; and by twelve, my first opera. In my brief life, I composed over six hundred works, including symphonies, masses, concertos, and operas, including *The Magic Flute*. I died in 1791, just before my thirty-sixth birthday.

Q.154 Howard Hughes

156

My father was a navy man, and we lived all over the country, which probably accounts for my skill at transforming myself into many characters: a mob lawyer, a country-western singer, or Joseph Stalin. I studied at New York's Neighborhood Playhouse, where my colleagues included Gene Hackman and Dustin Hoffman. In the 1970s, I was the original Frank Burns in *M*A*S*H*, and starred in George Lucas's first film. After several nominations, I won the Best Actor Oscar in 1983 for *Tender Mercies*.

157

An important figure in American military history, my remains lay forgotten in a Parisian grave before finally being moved to the U.S. Naval Academy Chapel in 1913, more than one hundred years after my death. I first went to sea at age twelve as a cabin boy. In 1773, while sailing in the West Indies, I killed a leader of a mutinous crew, but escaped before a trial was held, adding a phony last name (by which I'm now known) to escape detection by the British, who considered me a pirate. My ship, the *Bonhomme Richard,* defeated their *Serapis* in one of the most famous naval battles of the American Revolution, during which I told my crew I had not yet begun to fight.

Q.156 Robert Duvall

158

I came from a distinguished family in St. Paul, where I was named for a distant cousin, the writer of "The Star-Spangled Banner." At Princeton University, I developed a flair for writing and a taste for drink. My first book, *This Side of Paradise,* was published in 1920, which made my reputation as a gifted novelist and chronicler of the Jazz Age; I would follow it with *The Great Gatsby* and *Tender Is the Night.* Toward the end of my life I worked in Hollywood on film scripts, and died in 1940 before finishing *The Last Tycoon.*

159

I made several unsuccessful attempts to get my party's presidential nomination; ironically, I became vice president in 1974 without being elected. A year earlier, I'd resigned as New York's governor, a post I'd held for fourteen years. I was part of one of America's wealthiest families, a notable art collector, and was president of the Museum of Modern Art before entering politics.

Who Am I?

160

My successful methods of treating plague victims in France in the sixteenth century gained me a reputation as a great healer. Charles IX of France appointed me court physician, but today I am remembered for my book of predictions. Written in rhyme, *Centuries* tells of many future events (its accuracy is still debated), including the end of the world, in 3797 A.D.

161

The museum in my native Pittsburgh is one of only two in the United States devoted to a single artist. An odd, detached personality with a trademark white wig, I started off in advertising, before producing films (including three hours of a man sleeping), starting a magazine, and hosting my own talk show. I've designed album covers for John Lennon, the Rolling Stones, and the Velvet Underground (who got their start with me), and painted well-known portraits of Marilyn Monroe, Jackie Onassis, and numerous cans of soup.

162 During World War II, I worked in the government agency that later became the CIA, and was in charge of many top-secret documents. Although I am now one of America's most well-known culinary figures, I didn't study cooking until moving to Paris in my mid-thirties. My first book, *Mastering the Art of French Cooking,* was the best-selling cookbook of its day, and viewers got a taste of my down-to-earth style on my TV program *The French Chef.*

163

My name is associated with peace, but I made my fortune in explosives. I worked in St. Petersburg, Russia, and my native Sweden, trying to find a safe way to handle nitroglycerin, an extremely volatile substance. Using an organic packing material, I invented dynamite in 1867. Today, prizes are given out yearly in my name in many fields, including medicine, literature, and, yes, peace.

164 Although one of my famous novels deals with international intrigue on a submarine, I've never been to sea in one—in fact, my poor eyes kept me out of military service. While working at an insurance company in 1982, I wrote my first novel, *The Hunt for Red October*. Like many subsequent books, it was a military-oriented thriller, full of technical details and inside information, and became a best-seller and a film (and got a good review from President Reagan).

Who Am I ?

165

Talking has been my life: I gave recitations in church at an early age and was a news announcer on a local radio station while still in high school. In Baltimore and then Chicago, I hosted a local talk show that was later named for me and went into syndication. I'm now one of the most powerful people in entertainment (and one of only three women with a production studio); my shows feature celebrities, consumer and spiritual topics, and my popular book club. I also have my own magazine.

166

My march from Spain to Rome in 218–17 B.C. is considered one of the greatest military feats of all time. It involved forty thousand troops and several dozen elephants, used for both transportation and battle. Faced with hostile tribes, snow, and mudslides, we managed to make it over the Alps in fifteen days. Eventually, my Carthaginian army lost to Rome, and I took poison rather than surrender to the Romans.

167

167 In 1950, three years before my death, several hundred sportswriters and broadcasters voted me the outstanding athlete of the first half of the century. Born in Oklahoma in Indian territory, my Native American name was Wa-tho-huck, or "Bright Path." At the Carlisle Indian school, I excelled in football, hockey, swimming, and track and field (to name a few sports), and was on the Olympic team for track in 1912. Today, a town in Pennsylvania is named for me.

168

I was a renowned comic director, writer, and actor, and also wrote music for some of my films. Beloved by the public, I was also chastised by gossip columnists and journalists for my multiple marriages to women much younger than myself, and for my political stances (or lack thereof). My last wife was Eugene O'Neill's daughter, and we remained together for thirty-four years. In 1972, living in exile in Switzerland, I returned to the United States to receive a special Oscar.

169

Until my obituary ran in 1817, I was not known publicly as a novelist.

I didn't travel much, never married, and lived with my family for my entire life. My novels, exploring the lives and loves of the English upper classes, including *Emma* and *Pride and Prejudice*, have been filmed numerous times.

170

I was the first U.S. celebrity to speak out against the Vietnam War, supported civil rights, and appeared in a campaign commercial with Jacqueline Kennedy. But I was a trusted name years before that, thanks to my commonsense book of child care, which counseled parents to trust their intuition when raising their babies. I updated the book several times, incorporating nonsexist language and emphasizing the importance of fathers in a child's development. *Life* magazine has named me one of the hundred most important people of the twentieth century.

Q.170 Dr. Benjamin Spock

171

Eleven years before Rosa Parks refused to give up her seat on a bus to a white passenger, I was court-martialed for a similar offense while in the army. I was acquitted, and after my discharge spent several years playing ball for the Kansas City Monarchs in the Negro Leagues. After a decade in the majors, I was elected to the Hall of Fame my first year of eligibility. In October 1972, nine days before my death, I threw out the first pitch in the World Series, twenty-five years after integrating major league baseball.

172 I was a principal in a Roman Catholic school in Calcutta when I heard the calling to give up everything and work with the city's poor. In 1950, I founded the Missionaries of Charity, and received medical training in Paris so I could work with lepers and assist in natural disasters. When I received the Nobel Peace Prize in 1979, I said I was unworthy, but would accept in the name of the poor.

173

I explored space with a self-made telescope, discovering sunspots, the satellites of Jupiter, and the mountains and valleys of the moon. I changed the field of physics by describing the laws of falling bodies, and believed in precise measurements, rather than logic. For my belief that the earth moves around the sun, I faced opposition from the Catholic Church; I also angered philosophy professors, who agreed with Aristotle that no new object could exist in the universe. In 1992, 350 years after my death, the Vatican admitted it had made a mistake in condemning me.

174

In 1835, I was born with the arrival of Haley's comet, and I predicted (accurately) that I would leave this earth the next time it came around. I was a journalist, a riverboat captain (where I picked up my pen name), and wrote of my European travels in books like *The Innocents Abroad* and *A Tramp Abroad*. But I am best known for my novels, which include the tale of a mischievous boy and a runaway slave, and their odyssey down the Mississippi River.

175

Folksinger Woody Guthrie was a great influence on my work, and a song on my first album was dedicated to him. But my style was always changing, from folksinger, to protest singer, to electric rock poet, to country crooner. I've been one of rock's most influential artists, and everyone from Elvis to William Shatner has recorded my work. In the 1990s, I was inducted into the Rock and Roll Hall of Fame (by Bruce Springsteen); received a Kennedy Center honor; and won the Album of the Year Grammy for my 1997 CD *Time out of Mind*.

Who Am I ?

176

After selling paper cups and milkshake makers, I met a couple of brothers whose drive-in stand sold burgers, fries, and shakes quickly to hungry customers. I bought one of their franchises, then later acquired their whole business, keeping their last name, McDonald. Now a worldwide chain, it is estimated that 96 percent of the U.S. population eats there at least once a year, and we also buy 5 percent of the national potato crop for our fries.

To some, I am a Catholic martyr; to others, a rebel against the throne.

When I was only a week old, I was queen of Scotland, but after that country's war with England I was sent to France, where I was raised. In 1565, I married my English cousin in order to succeed Elizabeth I. When he died mysteriously two years later, I alarmed many of my supporters by marrying the man who'd allegedly murdered him. Elizabeth had me imprisoned, and she eventually signed my death warrant.

178

My next-to-last film, *The Swan*, was about a princess in love with a commoner, the opposite of my real-life romance. After a brief modeling career, I went to Hollywood, starred in several Hitchcock films, and won an Academy Award in 1954. I only made eleven films before my retirement. I married, and had three children: Albert, Stephanie, and Caroline.

179

By the time I was thirty, I had conquered most of the known world, from central Europe to India, and founded many cities—some estimates say more than sixty. My father was king of Macedonia, and when he was killed I inherited the throne. An influential military leader, perhaps the greatest of all time, I count Napoleon as just one of my disciples. I died in 323 B.C. of what was described as "a fever"; some say it was from too much wine.

180 I helped found the National Academy of Television Arts and Sciences, and was inducted into the Television Hall of Fame in 1984, ten years after my death. I began as a journalist, covering sports and then show business. My variety show, originally called *The Toast of the Town*, featured everyone from Dean Martin and Jerry Lewis (in their TV debuts) to opera singers to an Italian-accented mouse. I played a crucial role in introducing the Beatles to America and played myself in the film *Bye Bye Birdie*.

WHO AM I ?

181

I had a firsthand knowledge of oppressive regimes. My father was a diplomat, and we were forced to flee Czechoslovakia when the Nazis invaded, and later Yugoslavia, after a Communist coup. Although I'm accused of being undiplomatic, I say what I mean, unlike certain other members of my administration. The highest-ranking woman official in U.S. history, I was the U.S. representative to the United Nations before serving as secretary of state.

Q.180 Ed Sullivan

182

Initially, I had bad luck in my animation endeavors, and lost the rights to one of my creations, Oswald the Rabbit, in a contract dispute. But I created another character (first called Mortimer Mouse) who would become more successful. I've won twenty-six Academy Awards for my films, which include nature documentaries and live-action adventures as well as cartoons. My first theme park opened in 1955 in California, followed by others in Florida, France, and Japan.

Author Bio

I was born in Brooklyn in 1958, but a few years later moved to the New York suburbs. I've been writing for *Biography* since its inception, contributing reviews, features, and the *Who Am I?* column, as well as *Shocking, Lurid and True!,* which revisits famous scandals in history. In my spare time, I play music and write comedy and sometimes get paid for it.